Ancient Worlds

ROSANNE SWALWELL

Editorial Board
David Booth • Joan Green • Jack Booth

STECK-VAUGHN
Harcourt Achieve

www.HarcourtAchieve.com

10801 N. Mopac Expressway
Building # 3
Austin, TX 78759
1.800.531.5015

Steck-Vaughn is a trademark of Harcourt Achieve Inc. registered in the United States of America and/or other jurisdictions. All inquiries should be mailed to Harcourt Achieve Inc., P.O. Box 27010, Austin, TX 78755.

Rubicon © 2006 Rubicon Publishing Inc.
www.rubiconpublishing.com

All rights reserved. No part of this publication may be reproduced or transmitted in any form or by any means, electronic or mechanical, including photocopying, recording, taping, or any information storage and retrieval system, without permission in writing from the copyright owner.

Project Editors: Miriam Bardswich, Kim Koh
Editorial Assistant: Lori McNeelands
Art/Creative Director: Jennifer Drew-Tremblay
Assistant Art Director: Jen Harvey
Designer: Jeanette Debusschere

6 7 8 9 10   5 4 3 2 1

Ancient Worlds
ISBN 1-41902-393-4

CONTENTS

4 **Introduction**

6 **Amazing Facts**
Was pasta invented in Italy or China? The answer might surprise you. Learn about this and other amazing facts in these notes.

9 **Mesopotamia**
Check out these catchy headlines about life in Mesopotamia.

10 **The Mysterious Indus Valley**
What does a 4,000 year old flush toilet have to do with the Indus Valley? Find out in this article.

12 **Who's Your Mummy?**
Read this step-by-step list of how Egyptians mummified bodies and check out the report to find out why the mummy of a Buddhist monk wears sunglasses.

16 **Hunting for Treasure**
Gold, gold, and more gold! Learn all about the discovery of King Tut's tomb from the photographs and report.

20 **Daisy Dreamer — Cat Got Your Tongue**
Join Daisy Dreamer as she cracks down on crime in this graphic story.

23 **Queen Nefertiti**
What does a funny poem and a real-life missing person's account tell us about Queen Nefertiti? Check it out.

26 **The Second Son of Heaven**
Read about how the Kingdom of Mali was saved in this rainy-day story.

28 **Odysseus Meets the Cyclops**
One little man takes down one huge giant in this retelling of a legend.

32 **Statue Commits Murder**
Do you believe this? Read an unusual legend.

34 **Let the Games Begin**
Check out this historical account about the ancient Greek Olympics and Roman chariot races.

38 **Take Up the Sword of Justice!**
Adventure awaits you. Find out if you would fight beside Julius Caesar after reading this recruiting poster.

39 **The Terra Cotta Warriors**
Ever hear of soldiers made of clay? What about 7,500 soldiers? Learn the interesting details in this report.

42 **Rush For Freedom**
Hold tight while you read through the ups and downs of one Aztec slave's escape in this fictional story.

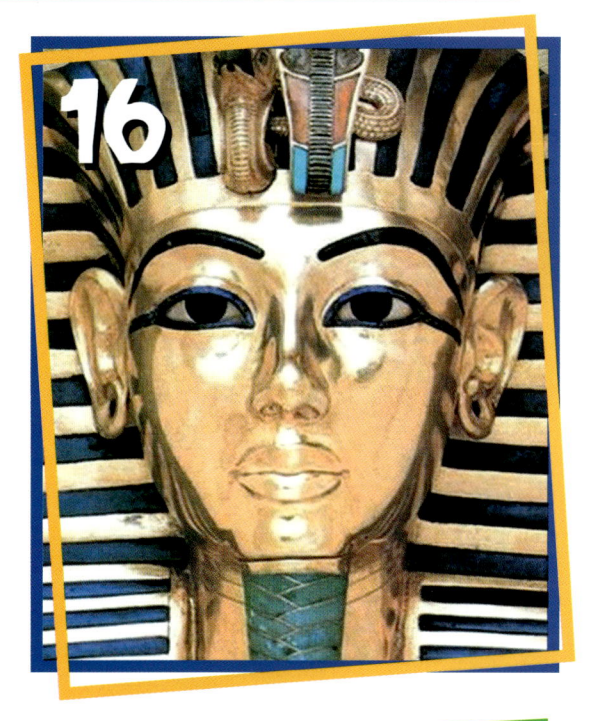

DIG IN

Uncover some *amazing facts* about the ancient world!

AMAZING FACTS

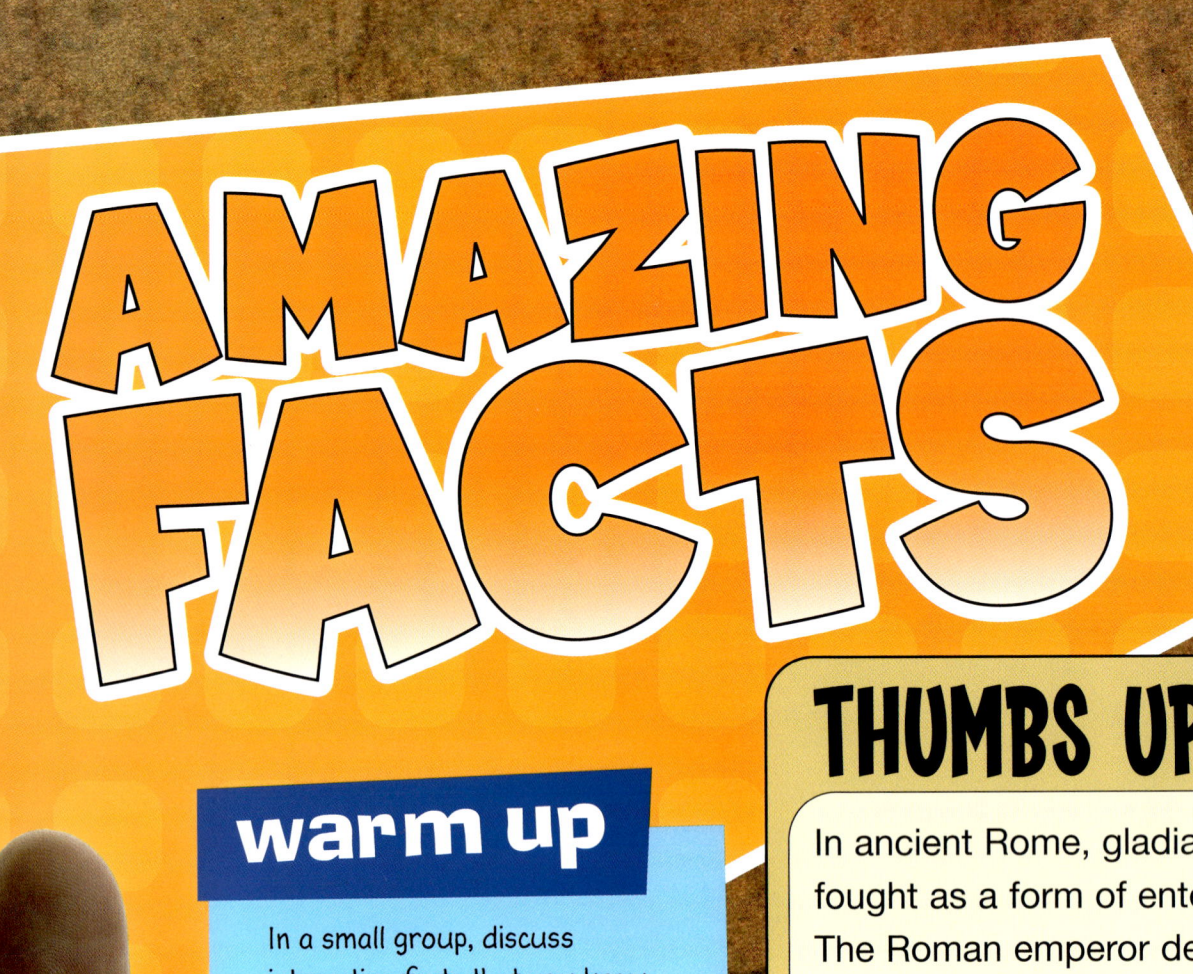

warm up
In a small group, discuss interesting facts that you know about the place where you live.

THUMBS UP!
In ancient Rome, gladiators fought as a form of entertainment. The Roman emperor decided if a gladiator lived or died. If the emperor gave a "thumbs up" signal, the gladiator lived. "Thumbs down" meant he was to be killed.

TIE THE KNOT
When two people in ancient Mexico got married, their clothing was tied together during the wedding ceremony. The saying, "tie the knot," came from this practice.

THE SUMMER MONTHS
The months July and August got their names from these ancient Roman emperors — Julius and Augustus Caesar.

All images–istockphoto

THANK YOU, CHINA

Most people think that pasta comes from Italy. Surprise! The people of China made pasta more than 3,000 years ago. They also invented: sunglasses, firecrackers, silk, paper, compasses, wheelbarrows, and even yummy ice cream!

HOOPS

A form of basketball was played by the ancient Mayans in Mexico and Central America. They used a hoop and a rubber ball but couldn't use their hands.

SPILL THE BEANS

In ancient Greece, club members decided who could join their club. They voted with beans. A white bean meant the person was welcome to join. A black bean meant the person was not welcome. Voters crossed hands as the beans were dropped into a darkened jar. This way no one knew how the vote was going. Today if you "spill the beans," it means that you are telling a secret.

TIME FOR SCHOOL

We can thank the Greeks for the idea of sending kids to school! Schools began in Athens, Greece, more than 2,000 years ago.

ALL ROADS LEAD TO ROME

This is a common saying and during the Roman Empire it was true. Many Roman roads can still be found beneath highways and roads in Europe.

FOOD FOR GODS

In ancient Mexico, chocolate was thought to be food for the gods. It was enjoyed at breakfast, lunch, and dinner. What would your mom say about this?

STONEHENGE

England's Stonehenge is made of stones that each weigh about 10,000 lb. It's amazing that ancient people were able to bring these stones from mountains 245 miles away. Think about how they might have done this.

wrap up

Which fact do you think is most amazing? Write an email to a friend telling him/her about it.

WEB CONNECTIONS

Use the Internet to find out more about one fact listed on this page. Share this information by designing a poster.

Mesopotamia

The Mesopotamians lived between two rivers — the Tigris and the Euphrates. Most of Mesopotamia was located in the present-day country of Iraq. Mesopotamia was a good name since it means "between the rivers."

warm up

This page has imaginary headlines for events in ancient Mesopotamia. Think about what we learn from headlines.

CHECKPOINT

Notice how headlines urge the reader to find out more about the subject.

This Just In: People Begin to Farm and Settle Down
7000 B.C.

New Invention Has Farmers Excited! It's Called a Wheel
5500 B.C.

Sumerians Take the Lead in Building First City
3500 B.C.

Largest Building Now Complete Ziggurat Wows Local Citizens! It's like a mountain with a temple on top
2800 B.C.

Walls Go Up! Sumerian Cities Protected From Raiders!
2500 B.C.

- Sumer was an area in southern Mesopotamia.

wrap up

1. Imagine you are a TV reporter. In a news announcer's voice, read the headlines to a group.

2. In a group, discuss how these inventions may have changed the lives of the people.

WEB CONNECTIONS

The Mesopotamians also invented writing. It was wedge-shaped and called cuneiform. Go to **www.upennmuseum.com/cuneiform.cgi**. Click on "your name in cuneiform." Make a drawing of your name using cuneiform symbols.

THE MYSTERIOUS INDUS VALLEY

warm up

Brainstorm the inventions that you use regularly, such as the telephone and the microwave oven. Discuss what people might have done before these inventions became part of our daily lives.

Thousands of years ago, flush toilets were unheard of in Europe. But they were in use over 4,000 years ago — in the Indus Valley.

Archaeologists were amazed at what else they found in the Indus Valley digs of Pakistan and western India. Two sites were special: Harappa and Mohenjo-Daro, cities of over 35,000 people!

Each city was planned! The streets were straight and lined with houses and shops. This is an important fact. No other towns or cities at that time had straight streets.

Scientists found pottery, beads, carts with wooden wheels, and ships with masts and sails.

archaeologists: *scientists who study artifacts (like pottery, drawings, and statues) from early people*

CHECKPOINT
Which do you think would be easier to plan, a straight road or a curved road? Why?

In Mohenjo-Daro, a magnificent bath was found in the center of the city. There were steps down to the pool and large verandas to provide shade for the bathers.

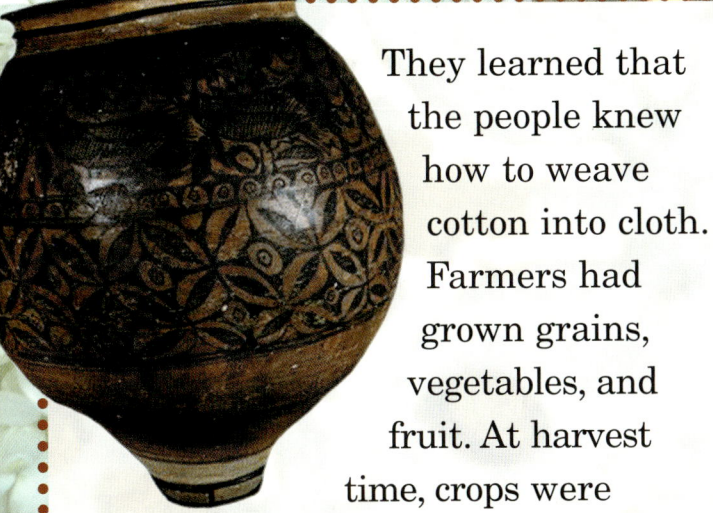

They learned that the people knew how to weave cotton into cloth. Farmers had grown grains, vegetables, and fruit. At harvest time, crops were brought to a central storage building and then distributed to the townspeople to eat.

CHECKPOINT
Notice how modern the Indus Valley was.

Here's where it gets really interesting! Many homes had built-in wells that provided fresh water for the family. There were bathrooms with flush toilets that connected to sewer pipes. Large pipes ran under the streets and took all the waste water from homes away to rivers. The Romans didn't have sewers for another 2,500 years!

Do you know what a seal is? A seal is made with a block of wood or stone, and markings are carved onto it. People often use them to stamp things they've made. Over 4,000 seals have been found in the Indus Valley.

Unfortunately, the Indus River flooded regularly. Each time it flooded, these great cities and all their advanced engineering would be wiped out. So new cities were built on top of the old ones. As time went on, less planning and talent went into building the cities. The most beautiful and best-planned city was found at the bottom of many other cities. Over time the people disappeared, as did their cities. We don't know why.

wrap up

1. Which Indus Valley invention do you think was most advanced? Explain your reasons in a sentence or two.

2. With a group, plan a small town. Where will you place shopping areas, parks, and public buildings like the police station or fire hall? Discuss reasons for your plan of the town with the class.

WEB CONNECTIONS

Using the Internet, visit the website: www.ancientindia.co.uk/indus/home_set.html. Scroll down to the bottom of the page and click on "Story." Read the story out loud to a friend.

WHO'S YOUR MUMMY?

warm up

With a group, make a list of things you already know about mummies. Then make a list of things you would like to know about them. Keep the list handy for changes after you've read this piece.

When people think of a mummy, they usually think of a body wrapped from head to toe in bandages, but this isn't always the case. Different people mummified the body in different ways. Some didn't use any bandages at all.

FYI

Ancient Egyptians left the heart in the mummy because they believed the soul needed it in the afterlife. Anubis, the god of the dead, would weigh it against a feather. If the heart was as light as a feather, the person would enjoy a happy afterlife. If the heart was heavy, the soul would be destroyed.

ANCIENT EGYPTIAN MUMMIES
3500 B.C. – 600 A.D.

Ancient Egyptians believed the body needed to be preserved so that the soul could identify the body in the afterlife. They preserved the body by mummifying it. This process was considered a religious ceremony, so it was performed by a priest.

1. The priest pulled the brain out through the nose using a hook.
2. Some organs were removed and placed into special jars called "canopic jars."
3. A cut was made in the lower left-side of the stomach. The intestines, stomach, liver, and lungs were pulled out through this hole.
4. The body was drained of fluids. This was done by stuffing the body with a salt-like substance called "natron." This would also be poured on top of the body. The body would stay covered for 40 days.
5. When the natron was removed, the body was stuffed with linens and covered with resin. Resin made the skin hard.
6. Finally, the body was wrapped from head to toe in clean linens and placed in a mummy casket.

This is an old drawing of Egyptians preparing a mummy.

CHECKPOINT
Why do you think the author wrote this information in a list? Do you think this makes the information easier to understand? Why?

preserved: *stopped from decaying*
resin: *a sap-like substance*

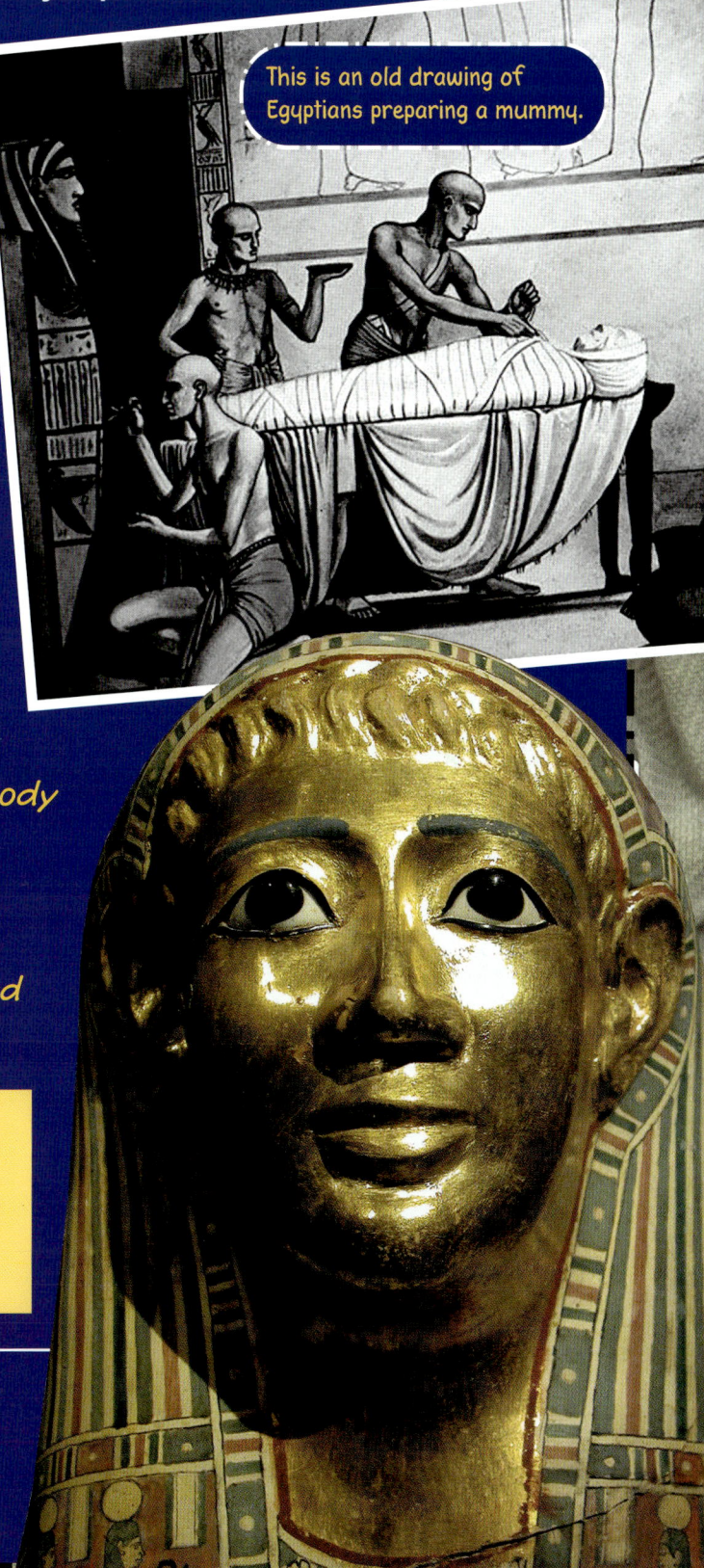

ASIAN MUMMIES
700 – 1000 A.D.

Would you believe that in ancient China, Japan, Thailand, and Vietnam the mummification process began before the person even died? It's true. When an important Buddhist monk was getting older, he gradually ate and drank less and less.

When he was very old, the monk moved into a special underground room lit only by smoky candles. The smoke helped to dry out his body.

This mummy of a child was found in China.

Once the monk died, the other monks finished drying out the body. Eventually, the mummified monk was put on display.

This mummified Buddhist monk is on display in Thailand. Sunglasses cover his dried-out eyeballs.

CHECKPOINT
Notice the reasons for creating a mummy.

FYI
The mummy of a Chinchorro tribesman was found in the Azapa Valley. The mummy was preserved by sand in approximately 8000 B.C. According to archaeologists, this is the first example of artificial mummification.

INCAN MUMMIES — SOUTH AMERICA
1100 – 1500 A.D.

In 1995, Dr. Reinhard was hiking across Mount Ampato in the Peruvian Andes, when he came across what he thought was a knapsack. It turned out not to be a knapsack at all — it was the mummy of a 14-year-old girl!

The Inca girl had been sacrificed by her community. The Incas often made human sacrifices to their gods. About 115 of these mummies have been found across South America.

These bodies were mummified by weather conditions, not on purpose. Extreme cold meant that the bodies would not decay after the person had died, and the strong, dry winds removed moisture from the body.

sacrificed: *killed as an offering to a god*

This mummy of an Incan girl is 500 years old.

wrap up

1. Imagine you are a world famous archaeologist. With a partner, prepare a small talk for a television interview about mummies. Present your interview to the class.

2. Mummies have been preserved for thousands of years. List two reasons we should still make mummies today, and two reasons we shouldn't.

WEB CONNECTIONS

Now that you've read how to make an Egyptian mummy, visit the website: www.bbc.co.uk/history/ancient/egyptians/mummy_maker_game.shtml to make your own virtual mummy!

HUNTING FOR TREASURE

warm up

Brainstorm the things that you and your friends think of as "treasure."

In Egypt, the pyramids or tombs of the ancient kings rise up from the desert like giant, pointed building blocks.

Howard Carter was certain one rock tomb was still undiscovered deep beneath the desert sand. He was determined to find it!

In 1922, Carter and his team of archaeologists set to work in a part of Egypt known as the Valley of the Kings. Almost all ancient pyramids and royal tombs are found there.

As the archaeologists dug, their shovels hit something hard! Excited, the team continued to dig, throwing the sand to the side. A huge stone step appeared. Carter grew even more excited. He knew from his earlier work that ancient tombs were marked by large entrance steps.

The digging continued. A second step was uncovered! Carter carefully examined each shovelful of sand.

CHECKPOINT
Why do you think Carter did this?

News of the discovery of the steps spread around the world. Carter was sure lost treasure was waiting under the steps.

On February 17, 1923, 16 steps had been swept clean. At the bottom of the steps was a door. Behind the door

Portrait of Howard Carter.

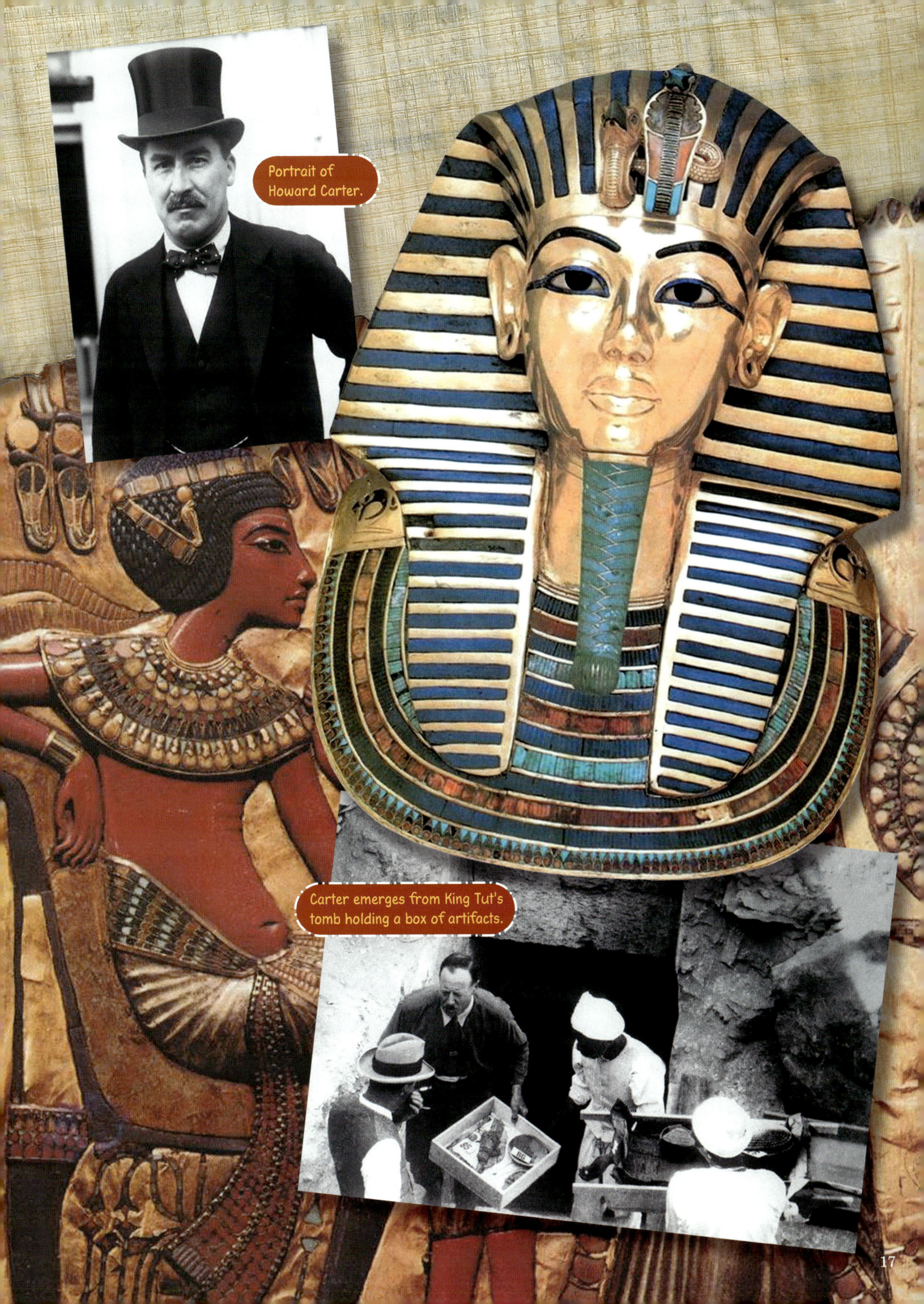

Carter emerges from King Tut's tomb holding a box of artifacts.

was a long hallway filled with rubble. Thieves had broken into the tomb!

> **CHECKPOINT**
> Predict how this story will end. Do you think the thieves left any treasure behind?

For two days, the men cleared the broken bits of pottery and statues. Suddenly a second door stood in front of them. The unmistakable *emblem* of an ancient Egyptian king was marked on the door.

Using his flashlight, Carter looked through a hole in the door while everyone waited to hear what he saw.

"Do you see anything?" the people asked.

"Yes, wonderful things," replied Carter.

Gold shimmered off the light from his flashlight. Heaps of treasure filled the room. Carter could see the king's large golden throne, full-size chariots, model ships and boats, life-like statues, and silver trumpets.

Two life-size statues stood by the door of the second room. Drawings of the ancient world covered three of the four walls. One wall was gold and had a door carved into its center. Carter couldn't believe his eyes — right in front of him lay a golden case shaped like a coffin.

Three cases, made of solid gold were opened. Hidden safely inside the last case was the body of King Tutankhamen (also known as King Tut). The king was hidden under a gold burial mask. The body was wrapped in layers of linen. Beautiful objects fell out as the layers were gently removed. When the last linen cloth was lifted away, Carter looked upon the face of a boy-king who had lived 3,253 years ago!

> **CHECKPOINT**
> Picture what Carter saw.

Newspaper reporters, tourists, and Egyptians joined the thousands of people waiting at the edge of the tomb, all hoping for a glimpse of the treasures and the body of the boy-king.

---

emblem: *symbol*

FYI

The curse of King Tut began when Lord Carnavron, who had paid for the discovery of the tomb, died soon after it was found. He had been bitten by a mosquito and the bite had become infected. However, Carter lived to 64, and thousands of visitors to the tomb have been fine.

View from inside King Tut's Tomb.

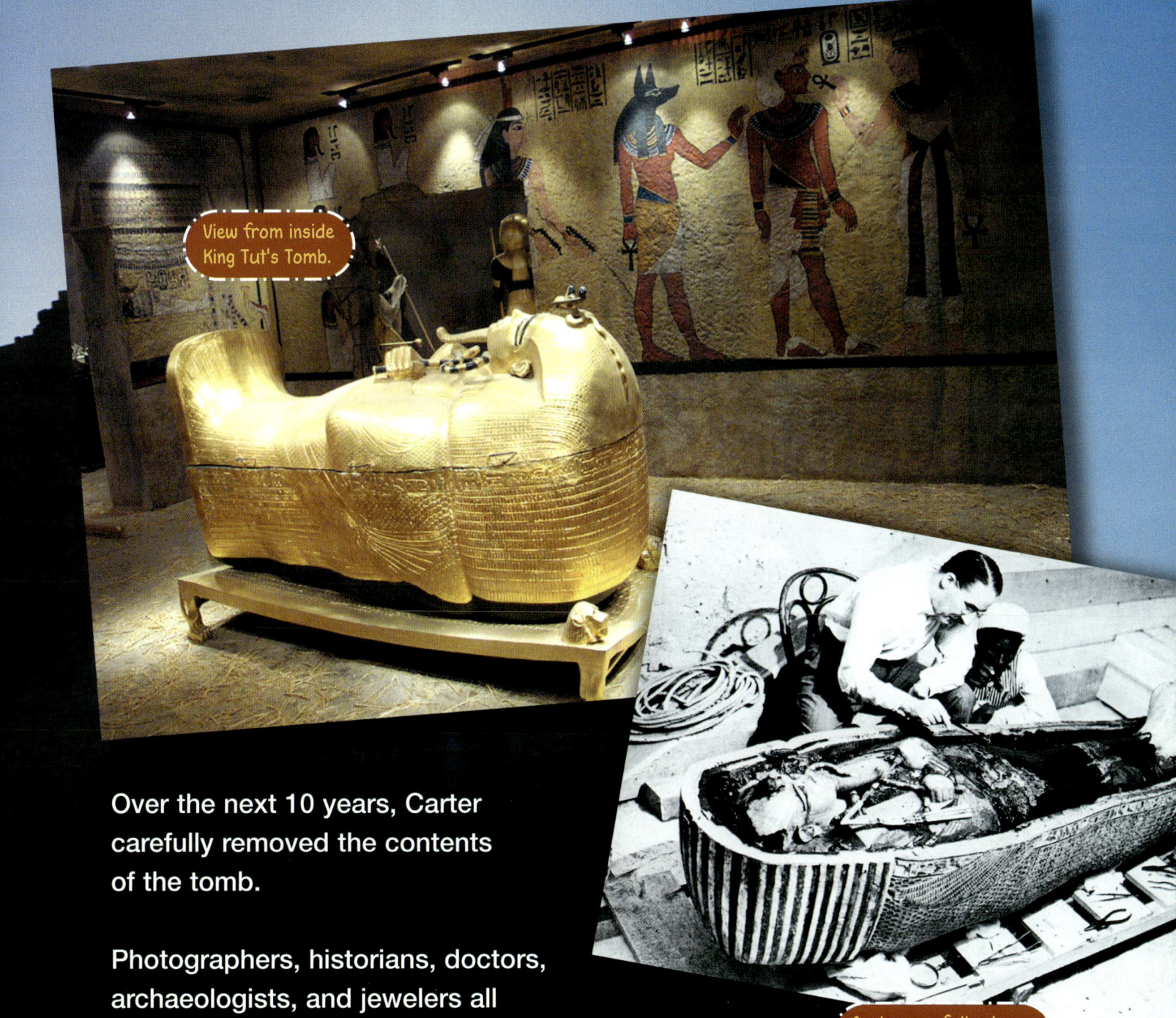

Carter carefully cleans King Tut's coffin.

Over the next 10 years, Carter carefully removed the contents of the tomb.

Photographers, historians, doctors, archaeologists, and jewelers all assisted Carter as they studied the contents of the tomb. Many of the treasures were taken to a museum in Cairo. But one item was not taken to the museum — King Tut's body remained in the burial room where the ancient Egyptians had left him.

FYI

Beside the burial room, the team discovered another space which held four small coffins. Each box contained one of King Tut's organs: his lungs, stomach, liver, and intestines.

wrap up

Design a poster announcing the discovery of King Tut's tomb. Include a description of the treasures, using bullets.

WEB CONNECTIONS

Go to **http://home.freeuk.net/elloughton13/** to learn more about King Tut. Design a bookmark with at least two pieces of information you discovered.

A twist of her cap leads to animal adventure

Daisy Dreamer

Cat Got Your Tongue

Ravi — Daisy's best pal
Annie — Daisy's other best pal
Dex — Daisy's dog

warm up

Look at the title of this story. What do you think this story will be about?

DAISY AND HER PARENTS ARE ON A CAMEL RIDE IN EGYPT. THEY'RE VISITING THE GREAT PYRAMID.

HOW DO YOU LIKE THE CAMEL RIDE?

IT'S ... BUMPY!

Illustrated by Gabriel Morrissette; colour—All Thumbs Creative/Peter Davis

DOES ANYONE LIVE INSIDE THE GREAT PYRAMID?
WHEN KING KHUFU DIED 4,500 YEARS AGO, HE WAS BURIED HERE. IT'S THE BIGGEST PYRAMID EVER BUILT!
I BET IT'S FULL OF TREASURE.
NOT ANYMORE, DAISY. ROBBERS STOLE MOST OF THE GOLD AND JEWELS.
GUIDE
BUT SOME PEOPLE BELIEVE THERE ARE STILL TREASURES HIDDEN INSIDE.
WHERE'S THAT LADY SNEAKING OFF TO?
SHE DISAPPEARED! I'M GOING TO SEE WHERE SHE WENT.
LOOKS LIKE SHE WENT INTO THIS SECRET ENTRANCE! MAYBE SHE'S LOOKING FOR TREASURE TO STEAL.
HA! THESE TREASURES WILL MAKE ME RICH!
I WAS RIGHT! I HAVE TO STOP HER.
DAISY TWISTS HER HAT AND BECOMES AN ANCIENT CAT STATUE!
CATS WERE SPECIAL IN ANCIENT EGYPT. PEOPLE BELIEVED CATS WERE GOOD LUCK. THAT'S WHY THEY MADE STATUES OF THEM.
IT'S TIME TO GIVE THIS THIEF A REAL SURPRISE!
?!
TAP TAP TAP
POKE

> HUH? THAT CAT STATUE! IT'S COME TO LIFE!

> HELLLLP!

> THE ROBBER SURE IS A SCAREDY CAT!

> DAISY TWISTS BACK INTO HERSELF.

> TIME TO GET BACK TO MOM AND DAD.

> THERE YOU ARE. WHAT WERE YOU DOING? DAYDREAMING ABOUT LIFE IN ANCIENT EGYPT?

> NO, I WAS PLAYING CATS AND ROBBERS!

wrap up

1. Why were cats special in ancient Egypt? In a sentence or two describe the cat statues.
2. Make up your own title for this story.

Ancient Egypt FACT

Ancient Egyptian kings were buried in pyramids when they died.

Queen Nefertiti

Spin a coin, spin a coin,
All fall down,
Queen Nefertiti
Stalks through the town.

Over the pavements
Her feet go clack.
Her legs are as tall
As a chimney stack.

Her fingers flicker
Like snakes in the air,
The walls split open
At her green-eyed stare.

Her voice is thin
As the ghosts of bees,
She will crumble your bones,
She will make your blood freeze.

Spin a coin, spin a coin,
All fall down,
Queen Nefertiti
Stalks through the town.

Anonymous

warm up

How would you describe Queen Nefertiti from the pictures you see on these pages?

The Real Queen Nefertiti

The real Queen Nefertiti was a beautiful woman as you can tell from the pictures on these pages. In fact, her name means "the beautiful woman has come." Her statue was carved around 1345 B.C. and is one of the most famous in the world.

CHECKPOINT

Notice Nefertiti's crown. She shaved her head so that it would fit snugly.

Queen Nefertiti was the wife of Pharaoh Akhenaton. She married him when she was only 12 years old. They had six daughters. When she was still very young, Nefertiti became the stepmother of King Tut.

Akhenaton and Nefertiti made an important royal decision while in power. All temples were to be destroyed. New temples, to honor the sun god, Ra, were built. Egyptians were forbidden to worship all gods but Ra. The priests became very angry with Akhenaton and Nefertiti.

This is Ra, the sun god.

This painting shows Pharaoh Akhenaton worshipping Ra.

The Missing Queen

Little is known about what happened to Queen Nefertiti. Did she die in childbirth? Was she killed by angry priests? Some scientists think she became the ruler of Egypt for a short time after King Tut died. Perhaps she made enemies and was sent far from the palace. We don't know. She's the missing queen. Even Nefertiti's mummy can't be found!

wrap up

1. With two or three partners, chant the poem *Queen Nefertiti* on page 23. Try saying it in different ways: whisper it, say it like a rap, say it slowly, say it fast. Tape your readings after some practice time. Play it for your group.

2. Create a missing person's flyer for Queen Nefertiti. Include a description of her, using bullets.

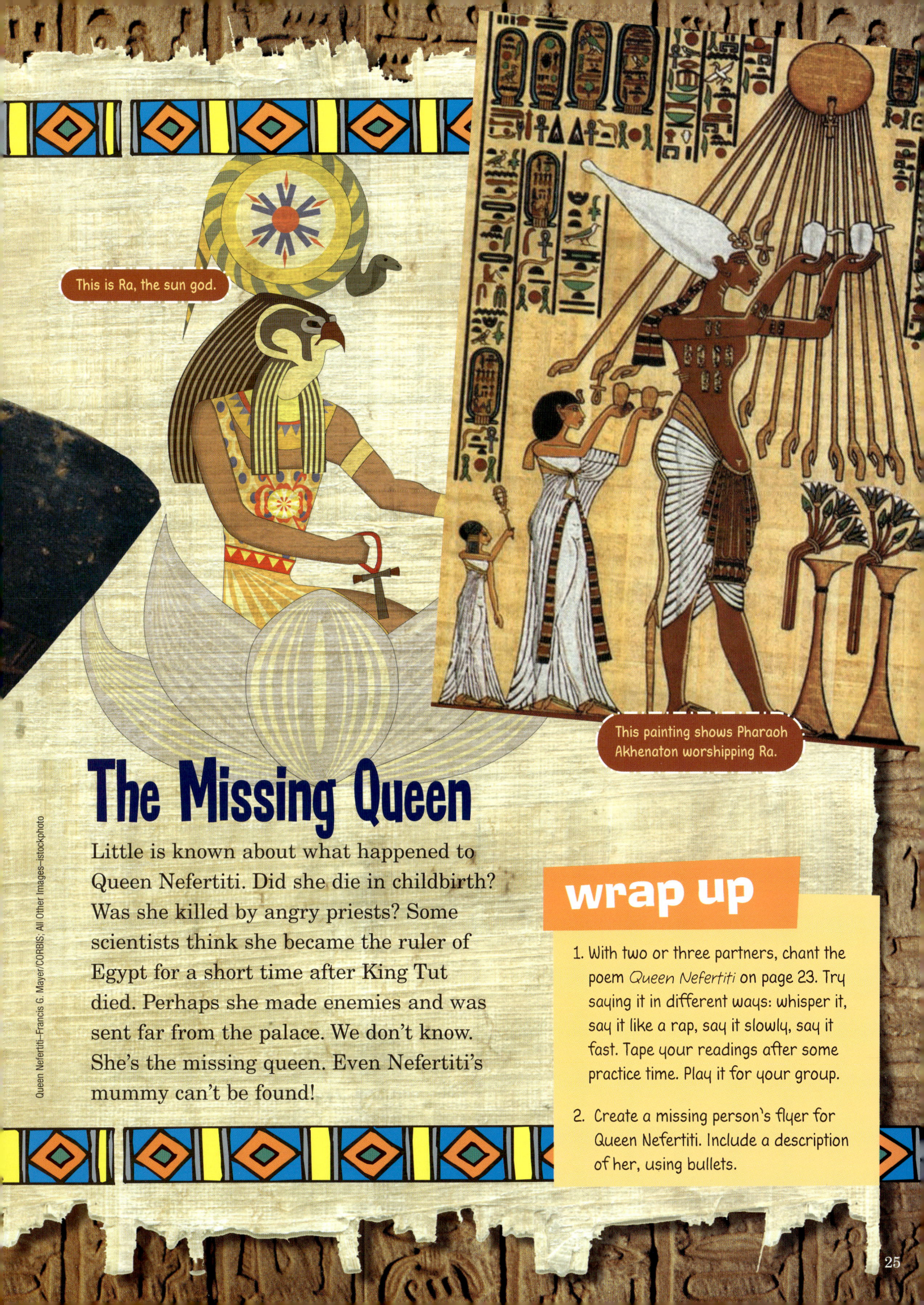

The Second Son of Heaven

warm up

Do your parents tell stories of you when you were very young? Think about one you might share with a friend. Listen as your friend tells you one from his or her life.

Mali, home of the real Lion King, was one of the earliest African empires. Griots or storytellers were important members of the Mali kingdom. Their stories kept the history and customs of their country alive. This is one of their stories.

Long ago Tano, the second son of Father Heaven, was sent to Earth to bring back sweet palm bread.

After following the path that links heaven to Earth, Tano came to a village of little round huts. He asked the chief for a loaf of sweet palm bread for Father Heaven. The chief was too busy preparing for a feast and sent Tano away with nothing but an angry look.

Tano went from village to village and everyone was too busy to listen to him.

He was ready to return to Father Heaven empty-handed when he spied a man walking along a trail. He asked for some sweet palm bread and right away the man brought Tano to his hut and gave him a freshly baked loaf of the bread. The second son of Father Heaven smiled.

"You must build a boat. Build it large, with no cracks for the water to come in. Gather your children and several pairs of animals and wait for my next visit," said Tano before he disappeared.

The man did as Tano asked. He built pens for as many animals as he and his family could find. Then he sat down and waited for Tano to return.

He waited and waited. Months went by. Finally, one night when the moon was a tiny sliver in the sky, Tano returned.

"Gather your family and the animals and get into the boat."

Soon rain began to fall. It filled the valleys and covered all the little round huts. But, the man, his family, and the animals were safe and dry.

After months and months of rain, Tano came to visit the man.

"The rain will end soon and the sun will return. The water will dry up, so make a bucket and collect the rainwater for you, your family, and the animals."

CHECKPOINT
Notice how each paragraph builds a picture. When the picture changes, a new paragraph begins.

The sun came out and shone brightly. The air grew drier and drier but the man, his family, and the animals were never thirsty. As soon as the bucket was empty, it filled up with water again.

Finally, the boat came to rest on the dried-out land. The man and his family built new little round huts and the animals ran and scampered all about.

Children and animals were born and grew in number. And even today whenever they eat sweet palm bread, the people look up to heaven and give thanks to Tano and to the old man who gave bread to the second son of Father Heaven.

wrap up
A griot is a storyteller not a story-reader. Reread the story about Tano and the sweet bread. With two or three friends, practice telling the story. When you are ready, tell the story to younger students.

WEB CONNECTIONS
Use the Internet to find out more about the ancient kings of Mali. Work with a friend to create a story about one of your discoveries.

Odysseus Meets the Cyclops

Adapted by Miriam Bardswich

warm up

Look at the pictures of the Cyclops on these pages. How would you describe the Cyclops?

This is a story from *The Odyssey*, by the Greek poet, Homer. Odysseus was a hero of the Trojan Wars.

On their voyage back to Greece, Odysseus and his men land on an island and set out to explore it. They come to a cave with a very high entrance. Inside the huge cave are large baskets of breads and cheeses, enormous bowls of fruit, giant pails of milk, and lambs wandering about.

"What wonderful stores! We can take them back to our ship," exclaims one sailor.

"No!" says Odysseus. "We wait for our hosts!"

A shadow falls across the entrance to the cave — that of a monster, large and hideous, with only one eye in the center of his forehead.

It's the Cyclops! The Greeks sit very still, cowering in the shadows.

The Cyclops picks up a huge flat stone and sets it across the mouth of the cave as a door.

Then he roars, "Strangers! Who are you? Come to steal from me?"

cowering: *shaking in fear*

CHECKPOINT

What do you think "stores" means here?

"We are Greeks," says Odysseus. "We have been fighting the Trojans for a long time. Now we are returning home. In the name of Zeus, we hope that you will show us kindness."

Seizing two of the sailors, the Cyclops throws them to the ground. "I don't care for Zeus or any of your gods! Poseidon is our only god. I'd as soon eat these two creatures."

Minutes later, the Cyclops drinks from a large bowl. "They were tasty. Now I'm full and tired."

While the Cyclops sleeps, the Greeks try to figure out how to move the stone from the doorway and sneak out of the cave.

CHECKPOINT
How do you think they will do this?

The next morning, the Cyclops leaves the cave, putting the stone back in place.

Odysseus spies the giant's huge staff, a tree trunk in the corner of the cave. "We'll cut off a piece, harden the end to make a stake that we can use as a weapon."

staff: *a pole used for walking or climbing*
stake: *a thick stick sharpened at one end*

That night, as the giant sits eating, Odysseus brings him something to drink. "Here, this will make your food taste better."

Cyclops: "What is your name?"

Odysseus: "Nobody."

Cyclops: "Then I shall eat you last, Nobody."

While the Cyclops is sleeping, Odysseus and his men take their weapon and put the end into the fire. They plunge the end of it into the eye of the Cyclops. The Cyclops howls with pain.

Outside the cave door, two other Cyclops call out, "Who is hurting you, Polyphemus?"

CHECKPOINT
Notice that Cyclops is spelled the same way for the singular and plural nouns.

"Nobody is hurting me."

"Then, if nobody is hurting you, stop yelling."

The injured Cyclops moves to the doorway, hands outstretched. "It's cooler here."

Sheep, tied together in threes, and with sailors clinging underneath their bellies, pass under the arms of the Cyclops.

Odysseus and his men race across the fields. "Hurry," shouts Odysseus, "before he figures it out."

wrap up

1. How do the sailors react when they see the Cyclops? Write a short dialogue that two sailors might have whispered to each other when they first saw him.

2. With a partner, create two frames for a storyboard to finish this story.

Statue Commits MURDER

warm up

As a class, share what you know about famous statues. Do you think it's important for a city to have statues? Why or why not?

Long ago, there lived a man called Theagenes. He was from the island of Thasos. Theagenes was a champion boxer, a great runner, and a superman. In fact, he was so important that the citizens of Thasos thought a statue should be made in his honor. And so it was.

Everyone loved Theagenes. Well, not quite everyone. One man in Thasos didn't like Theagenes at all. Each night he would sneak into town and beat the statue! One dark night, the statue toppled over and killed him instantly.

The victim's sons accused the statue of murder. It was found guilty! As punishment the statue was *exiled* and thrown into the sea.

CHECKPOINT
How would you have treated the statue?

exiled: sent away from a home or country

Time passed. A **famine** struck the island of Thasos. The hungry citizens traveled all the way to Delphi, to ask an **oracle** for help. The oracle said the famine would stop when all the exiles returned to the island.

The citizens did as they were told, but the famine continued. They returned to Delphi, where a great priestess reminded them that the bronze statue of Theagenes had not been returned to the island. The people traveled home as fast as they could, but they couldn't find the statue.

famine: *extreme shortage of food*
oracle: *person who gives advice*

The famine continued. One day a group of fishermen pulled their nets into their boat and stuck in the net was the statue. The great statue of Theagenes was returned to its place. The famine ended. Just like that!

wrap up

1. Write a headline for a newspaper article about what happened the night the murder/death took place.

2. Design a stand that would keep the statue from falling and hurting tourists.

LET THE GAMES BEGIN

warm up

Have you or your team ever competed for a medal or trophy? What did you do to prepare yourself? How did you feel when you won or lost?

THE OLYMPICS

Today, whenever the Olympic Games are held, people from all over the world stay glued to the television. For two weeks, the whole world shares one common focus — the Games!

Would you believe that this very special tradition began in ancient Greece? It's true. The first Olympics (that we have written records of) took place in 776 B.C. Now that was a long time ago!

The games were different then. Athletes represented themselves, not a country as they do today.

CHECKPOINT

Do you think this was a good idea? Should that still happen today?

And they did it in the nude! That's right — athletes in the very first Olympic Games did not wear special clothing to compete. Instead, they didn't wear any clothing at all.

Much like today, the ancient Olympics were a very special event. The Greeks actually started the Games to honor their gods. They believed that fighting would disappoint the gods, so for one month all war and fighting stopped. Many soldiers even became athletes during this time of peace. After the Games, soldiers could travel back to the battleground without concern that they might be attacked.

The Olympics were held every four years just as they are today. But in the beginning, only one competition was held. It was a foot race. Gradually, the Games included other events such as, chariot racing, boxing, and wrestling.

When athletes won events, their skills and hard work were rewarded. They were given crowns made from olive leaves. Statues were also made in their honor.

Today, wars may not stop and athletes may not be naked, but everyone still cheers when the Olympics roll around every four years.

FYI

Only men, boys, and unmarried women were allowed to watch the games. If slaves, girls, or married women were caught attending, they would be severely punished by the law.

CHARIOT RACING IN ROME

In ancient Rome, chariot racing drew large crowds to the circus or arena. The largest arena, the Circus Maximus, could hold as many as 250,000 people. Today, the largest arena holds about 120,000 people.

The races were great occasions. People dressed in their finest clothes, often in team colors — red, white, blue, and green.

Chariots were pulled by two or four horses. They raced around the arena seven times at very fast speeds. Sometimes chariots tipped over and drivers were trampled. At other times chariots crashed into one another. Drivers had to have great skill to avoid accidents. Some of the best drivers even raced ten horses together when they wanted to show off.

This is a scene from the movie *Ben Hur*, made in 1959.

wrap up

1. Imagine you and a friend are attending an Olympic event in ancient Greece or a chariot race in Rome. Write a diary entry about your experience.

2. Create a poster to announce the ancient Olympic Games (be sure to mention the time of truce) or an upcoming Roman chariot race.

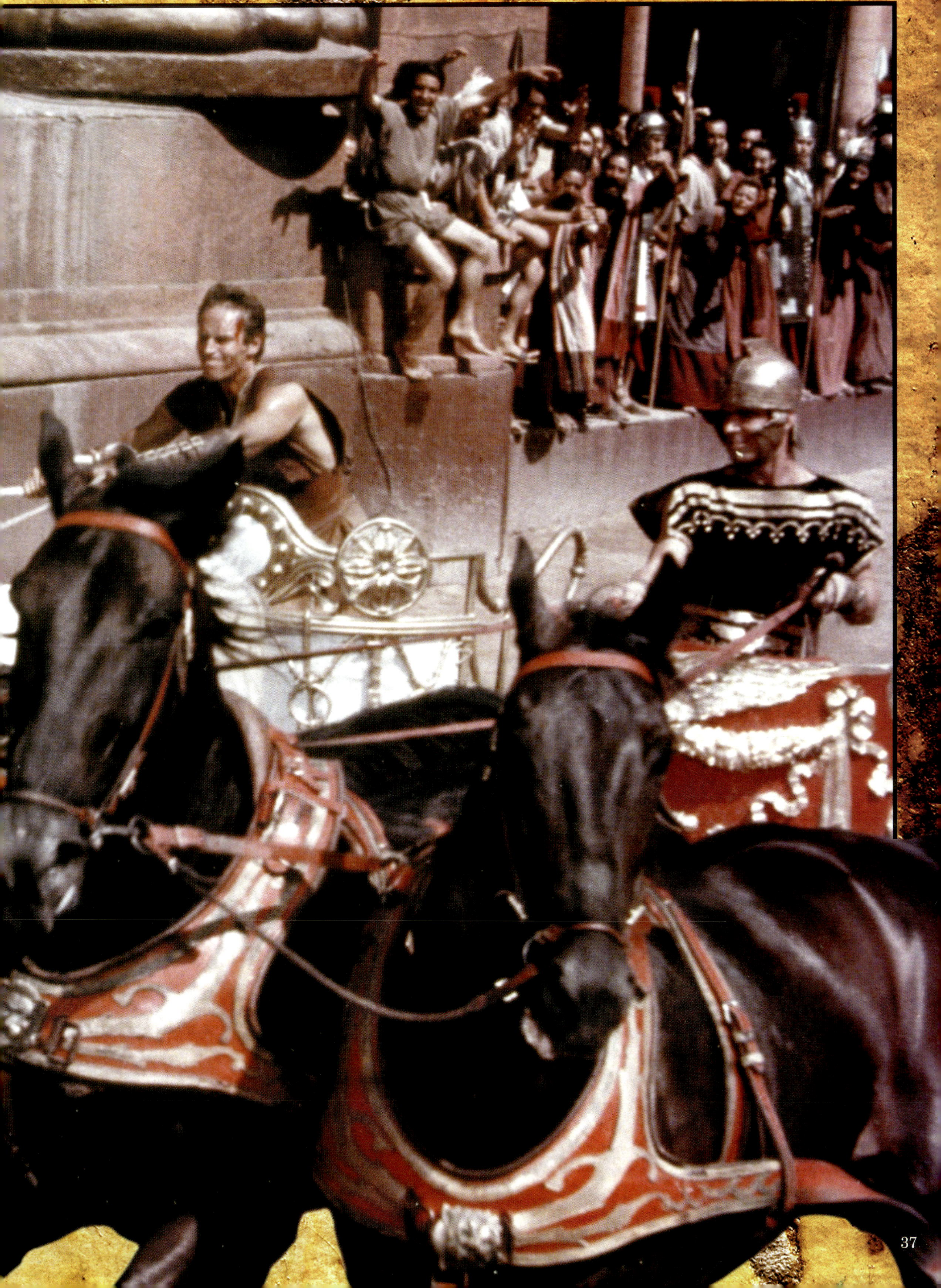

Take Up the Sword of Justice!

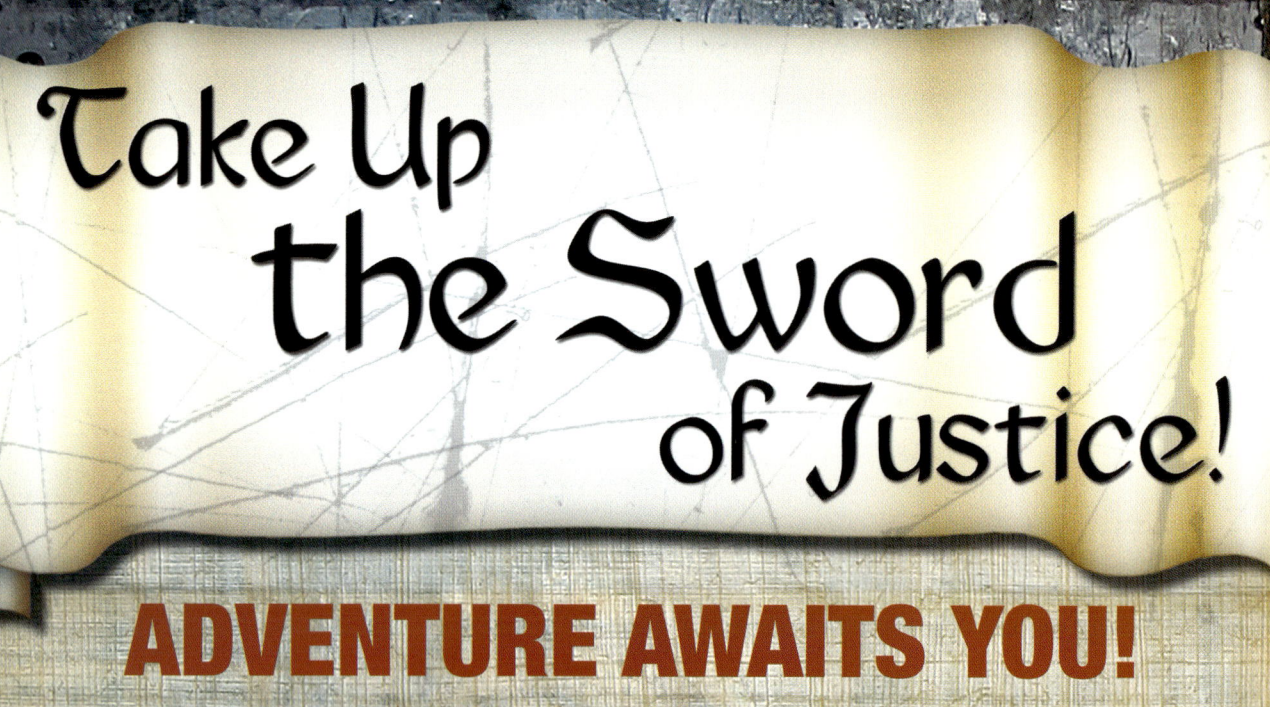

ADVENTURE AWAITS YOU!

Fight beside Julius Caesar — the greatest soldier today!

Journey over mountains, seas, and deserts.
Earn one denarius a day.
Get three great meals daily.
Enjoy free fitness training.
Gain the respect of friends and family!

ENLIST TODAY

The Roman Empire Needs You!

wrap up

Go to the library or visit www.historyforkids.org to find out more about Julius Caesar. When did he live? What countries did he conquer? Make a travel brochure for the countries.

warm up

Using modeling clay, make a human face. How will you make it look real?

In 1974, the wells near Shaanxi, China, were drying up. Farmers in the area began to search for a new source of water.

They came upon a hill with trees growing nearby and began to dig. Their shovels struck something very hard. As they dug further, they discovered it wasn't a stone but a head! The farmers continued to dig and found a full-size clay soldier dressed in ancient armor. The astonished farmers called the local government to tell them about their discovery.

THE TERRA COTTA WARRIORS

The Eighth Wonder of the World

At Attention!

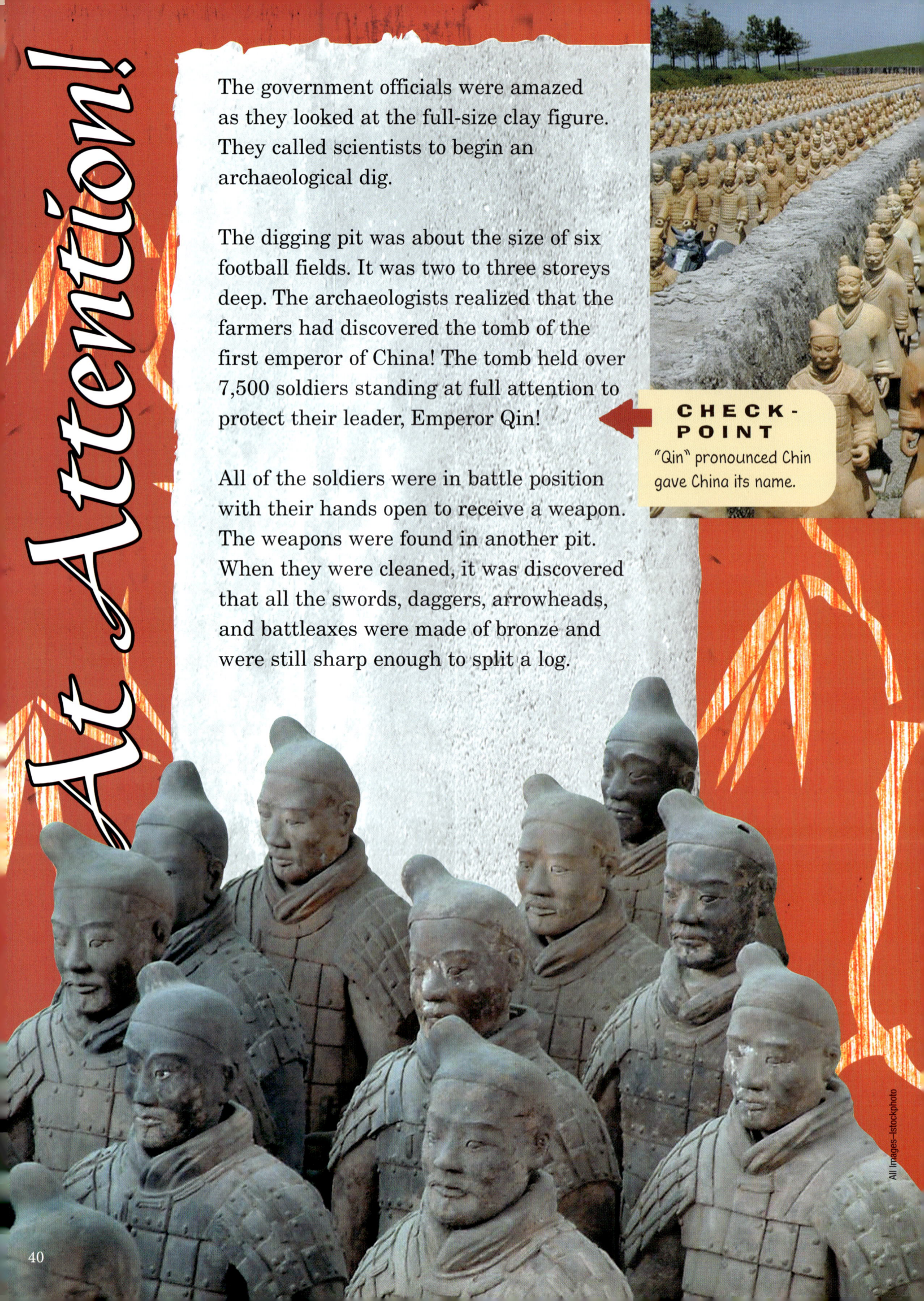

The government officials were amazed as they looked at the full-size clay figure. They called scientists to begin an archaeological dig.

The digging pit was about the size of six football fields. It was two to three storeys deep. The archaeologists realized that the farmers had discovered the tomb of the first emperor of China! The tomb held over 7,500 soldiers standing at full attention to protect their leader, Emperor Qin!

All of the soldiers were in battle position with their hands open to receive a weapon. The weapons were found in another pit. When they were cleaned, it was discovered that all the swords, daggers, arrowheads, and battleaxes were made of bronze and were still sharp enough to split a log.

CHECK-POINT
"Qin" pronounced Chin gave China its name.

Every soldier had been made of terra cotta clay and baked in a fire-hot kiln. They became known as the Terra Cotta Warriors.

As more and more warriors were uncovered, the archaeologists noticed that each soldier had its own facial expression. Even the uniforms were different for each rank of soldier. The warriors wore black or brown armor over uniforms painted red or green. The heads and hands of all the warriors were removable and could be exchanged.

terra cotta: *brownish-red clay*
kiln: *oven*

FYI

- The soldiers were life-size, ranging in height from 5 ft. 5 in. to 6 ft. 5 in. Each weighed more than 400 lb. As the dig continued, clay horses and chariots were also found.
- Deadly booby traps were planted around the tomb.

wrap up

1. Imagine you were one of the potters commanded to make the Terra Cotta Warriors. In your journal, record the instructions given to you and what happened as you built the emperor's tomb.

2. Draw a Venn diagram and compare the Terra Cotta Warriors to today's soldiers.

WEB CONNECTIONS

Use pictures of the Terra Cotta Warriors from the Internet to create a travel poster.

warm up

Think of a situation that forced you to take a risk of some kind. Was the end result worth the risk? If you could go back in time, would you take the same chance again?

RUSH FOR FREEDOM

By Robert Piotrowski

After the man with the gold bracelets pays the merchant, I am pushed off to the side with the other slaves. All around us buyers and sellers continue their work. The man with the gold bracelets has bought me. He is my master now.

My name is Running One Rabbit. I am an Aztec. I come from a family of farmers. But, from today I am a slave.

My master is coming my way.

I shuffle my feet. They feel ready. I pull at the rope that binds my hands together. It loosens a little. It is difficult to run with your wrists tied.

Illustrated by Mike Rooth

And soon I will run like a jaguar was at my heels. A big, fat jaguar with shiny gold spots.

I begin running toward my master.

He guesses what I am planning. He stops in the aisle between the slave merchant and a cage of young dogs. This leaves me little room for escape.

My bare feet pound on the floor of the marketplace. My arms, still tied, pump together before me. I hope I do not fall before I reach him.

> **CHECKPOINT**
> What does the master look like?

It takes me ten **strides**. My master is only half a head taller than me, but twice as wide. He might as well be a mountain. My freedom lies behind him.

Aztec law states that a slave sold at the marketplace who escapes and reaches the emperor's palace is given freedom. But first I must get by my master. He is the only one who can stand in my way, unless he has a son. Under the law, no one else is allowed to stop me.

> **CHECKPOINT**
> What is Running One Rabbit planning? Who stands in his way?

At the last moment, I **veer** to the right to avoid my master. My idea is to get past him by jumping clear over the cage of dogs. I am a good jumper. I leap as high and far as I can.

---

strides: *long steps*

veer: *turn*

My attempt fails.

My master catches my elbow and draws me toward him. But I am smarter than he. Instead of struggling in mid-air, I purposely fall into him. I stick my elbows and knees out hoping to catch him in a soft place.

It works. We topple to the ground together. In the confusion, my master lets go of my arm. I jump to my feet and run, run, run.

A great joy overtakes me. I am so full of energy that I only half realize my bonds were broken during our tumble. I can still hear him yelling as I pass merchants selling canoes and copper tools.

"Ten Crocodile! Ten Crocodile, come to me! To me!" he screams. What a fool. My master thinks he knows my name. Even if he does, I would not return to him. I want to be free!

> **CHECKPOINT**
> Running One Rabbit has gotten past his new master but his escape is not complete. What else does he need to do before he is free?

I pause for a moment. I know Emperor Montezuma's palace is not far, but I don't know which direction to take.

I decide to go left because that way is less crowded. I doubt my master will be able to catch up to me. I am a good runner. Still, I must be careful. And, I must hurry!

I run for what feels like a thousand moments. My mouth is dry. My legs scream for rest.

I stumble once. Then again, almost tripping. I cannot stop now. Not until I find the palace.

Suddenly, I am on the ground. My ankle screams in pain. It is sprained. My run is over. I can go no farther.

Then I see the palace. It is right in front of me. A hundred steps away. All I have to do is get up and walk to it. Then I will be free.

I struggle to my feet. My ankle is sore but strong enough to hold my weight. I limp in the direction of the palace.

Then a giant steps in front of me.

No, it is only a man. A boy. He looks older than me. He is not tall but wide and thick. His face is wet with sweat. His broad chest heaves like he too has been running. But what does he want? Why does he stand in my way?

"I am Ten Crocodile. You are my father's slave. And that is what you will remain. I will not let you get to the palace and win your freedom."

Of course! I am such a fool. When the man with the gold bracelets was yelling, he was not calling me. Instead he was yelling for this boy, his son. Aztec law says he too can catch me before I reach the palace. And now, here he stands blocking my way to freedom.

CHECKPOINT

Why does Running One Rabbit seem to be more afraid of Ten Crocodile than he was of the man with the gold bracelets?

---

heaves: *rises*

Pain shoots up my leg as I shift my weight onto my sprained ankle. Ten Crocodile smiles. He thinks I will be easy prey.

I try not to think about the pain. Instead I think about my family and farming in the hot sun. I remember that I am no one's slave. I am Running One Rabbit.

Suddenly, I am running toward the figure standing between me and the palace. I am not thinking about what I will do when I reach him. I am still thinking about my family and freedom.

Ten Crocodile digs his feet into the dirt. I am almost upon him. He crouches. His thick arms are set for attack. He will come for me from below. It is a clever plan. But it will not be successful.

CHECKPOINT
Notice what Running One Rabbit does.

As I expect, Ten Crocodile lunges at my feet. At the last moment I throw myself into the space above him. His powerful arms catch only air. I soar over top of them.

---

prey: *someone's victim*
lunges: *moves forward quickly*

I am jumping over his back. And so the rabbit outsmarts the crocodile.

I land on my good leg and continue running for the palace. My next step sends another jolt of pain from my ankle. I ignore it and run like I have never run before. I am almost there. I think about Ten Crocodile chasing after me. Reaching out. Pulling me down to the ground. Ending my escape for freedom and making me his father's slave.

But he does not. Cannot. Instead, Ten Crocodile lies in the dirt, watching this rabbit run to freedom.

FYI

Aztecs had many laws that protected slaves. For example, their masters had to provide them with food and shelter.

wrap up

1. With a partner, discuss how Running One Rabbit outsmarts the master's son.

2. In a group, create a storyboard about Running One Rabbit's first day of freedom. How does he feel? Where does he go? What does he do there? Whom does he meet?

WEB CONNECTIONS

Using the Internet, go to **http://library.thinkquest.org/27981/** to learn more about the Aztecs. Pick one topic and report your findings to the class.

ACKNOWLEDGMENTS

The publisher gratefully acknowledges the following for permission to reprint copyrighted material in this book.

Every reasonable effort has been made to trace the owners of copyrighted material and to make due acknowledgment. Any errors or omissions drawn to our attention will be gladly rectified in future editions.

"Daisy Dreamer" adapted from *chickaDEE magazine*, "Daisy Dreamer: Cat Got Your Tongue" November 2003 by Philip Moscovitch. Illustrations by Gabriel Morrissette. Used with permission of Bayard Presse Canada Inc.

Statue Commits Murder adapted from www.digonsite.com web site, © 2005, Cobblestone Publishing, 30 Grove Street, Suite C, Peterborough, NH 03458. All Rights Reserved. Reprinted by permission of Carus Publishing Company.